For exams in 2025

ICAEW
Financial Accounting and Reporting – UK GAAP

Eighth edition 2024

ISBN 9781 0355 1905 7

eISBN 9781 0355 1918 7

British Library Cataloguing-in-Publication Data

A catalogue record for this publication is available from the British Library

Published by

BPP Learning Media Ltd,
BPP House, Aldine Place,
142-144 Uxbridge Road,
London W12 8AA

www.bpp.com/learningmedia

Printed in the United Kingdom

Your learning materials, published by BPP Learning Media Ltd, are printed on paper obtained from traceable sustainable sources.

All rights reserved. No part of this publication may be reproduced, stored in a retrieval system or transmitted, in any form or by any means, electronic, mechanical, photocopying, recording or otherwise, without the prior written permission of BPP Learning Media.

The content of this publication is intended to prepare students for the ICAEW examinations, and should not be used as professional advice. Although every effort has been made to ensure that the contents of this book are correct at the time of going to press, BPP Learning Media makes no warranty that the information in this book is accurate or complete and accepts no liability for any loss or damage suffered by any person acting or refraining from acting as a result of the material in this book.

ICAEW takes no responsibility for the content of any supplemental training materials supplied by the Partner in Learning.

The ICAEW Partner in Learning logo, ACA and ICAEW CFAB are all registered trademarks of ICAEW and are used under licence by BPP Learning Media Ltd.

BPP Learning Media Ltd
2024

BPP Learning Media is grateful to the IASB for permission to reproduce extracts from IFRS® Accounting Standards, IAS® Standards, SIC and IFRIC. This publication contains copyright © material and trademarks of the IFRS Foundation®. All rights reserved. Used under license from the IFRS Foundation®. Reproduction and use rights are strictly limited. For more information about the IFRS Foundation and rights to use its material please visit www.IFRS.org.

Disclaimer: To the extent permitted by applicable law the Board and the IFRS Foundation expressly disclaims all liability howsoever arising from this publication or any translation thereof whether in contract, tort or otherwise (including, but not limited to, liability for any negligent act or omission) to any person in respect of any claims or losses of any nature including direct, indirect, incidental or consequential loss, punitive damages, penalties or costs.

Information contained in this publication does not constitute advice and should not be substituted for the services of an appropriately qualified professional.

Copyright © IFRS Foundation

All rights reserved. Reproduction and use rights are strictly limited. No part of this publication may be translated, reprinted or reproduced or utilised in any form either in whole or in part or by any electronic, mechanical or other means, now known or hereafter invented, including photocopying and recording, or in any information storage and retrieval system, without prior permission in writing from the IFRS Foundation. Contact the IFRS Foundation for further details.

The Foundation has trade marks registered around the world (Trade Marks) including 'IAS®', 'IASB®', 'IFRIC®', 'IFRS®', the IFRS® logo, 'IFRS for SMEs®', IFRS for SMEs® logo, the 'Hexagon Device', 'International Financial Reporting Standards®', NIIF® and 'SIC®'.

Further details of the Foundation's Trade Marks are available from the Licensor on request.

| | Preface | Contents |

Welcome to BPP Learning Media's **Passcards** for ICAEW **Financial Accounting and Reporting – UK GAAP.**

- They **save you time**. Important topics are summarised for you.
- They incorporate **diagrams** to kick start your memory.
- They follow the overall **structure** of the ICAEW Workbook, but BPP Learning Media's ICAEW **Passcards** are not just a condensed book. Each card has been separately designed for clear presentation. Topics are self-contained and can be grasped visually.
- ICAEW **Passcards** are **just the right size** for pockets and bags.
- ICAEW **Passcards focus on the exams** you will be facing.

Run through the **Passcards** as often as you can during your final revision period. The day before the exam, try to go through the **Passcards** again! You will then be well on your way to passing your exams.

Good luck!

		Page			Page
1	Reporting framework	1	13	Consolidated balance sheet	105
2	Ethics and sustainability	9	14	Consolidated statements of financial performance	111
3	Format of financial statements	15	15	Associates and joint ventures	117
4	Reporting financial performance	27	16	Group accounts: disposals	123
5	Tangible fixed assets	43	17	Group statement of cash flows	129
6	Intangible fixed assets	53	18	Micro-entities	135
7	Revenue and inventories	61	19	IFRS Accounting Standards overview	141
8	Leases	65			
9	Financial instruments	71			
10	Other issues	81			
11	Analysis and interpretation of financial and non-financial information	89			
12	Group accounts: basic principles	97			

Notes

1: Reporting framework

Topic List

Financial statements

Purpose and use of financial statements

Bases of accounting

FRS 102 Section 2 *Concepts and Pervasive Principles*

The UK *Regulatory Framework*

Inherent limitations of financial statements

In order to properly appreciate FRS 102 it is important to understand the reporting framework which underlies this standard.

Tabs: Financial statements | Purpose and use of financial statements | Bases of accounting | FRS 102 Section 2 | The UK *Regulatory Framework* | Inherent limitations of financial statements

Objective of financial statements

> To provide information about the financial position, performance and cash flows of an entity that is useful for economic decision-making by a broad range of users.

Financial statements are used to make economic decisions, such as:

- to decide when to buy, hold or sell an equity investment;
- to assess the stewardship or accountability of management; and
- to assess security for amounts lent to the entity.

| Financial statements | **Purpose and use of financial statements** | Bases of accounting | FRS 102 Section 2 | The UK *Regulatory Framework* | Inherent limitations of financial statements |

Financial position
- balance sheet

→ Helps users assess entity's financial strengths/weaknesses, including liquidity and solvency and likely needs for financing.

Financial performance
- profit and loss account
- statement of changes in equity

→ Helps users understand the return the entity has produced on its economic resources. Indicator of how efficiently/effectively resources have been used.

Cash flows
- statement of cash flows

→ Helps users assess entity's ability to generate future net cash inflows, gives users a better understanding of operations.

| Financial statements | Purpose and use of financial statements | **Bases of accounting** | FRS 102 Section 2 | The UK *Regulatory Framework* | Inherent limitations of financial statements |

FRS 102 sets out three bases of accounting:

1 Accrual basis – transactions are recognised when they occur, not when the related cash flows take place.

2 Cash basis – not allowed under UK GAAP to prepare the profit and loss account but may be used for small unincorporated entities. Cash basis is obviously the basis used to prepare the statement of cash flows.

3 Break up basis – used where there is an intention or need to sell off the assets of the business. The break-up basis values assets and liabilities today as if the entity was about to cease trading.

The going concern basis is assumed to apply unless the entity has disclosed otherwise.

FRS 102 recognises the following qualitative characteristics of financial information:

- understandability
- relevance
- materiality
- reliability
- prudence
- substance over form
- completeness
- comparability
- timeliness
- balance between benefit and cost

Information that possess these qualitative characteristics will be useful to users in making economic decisions about the entity.

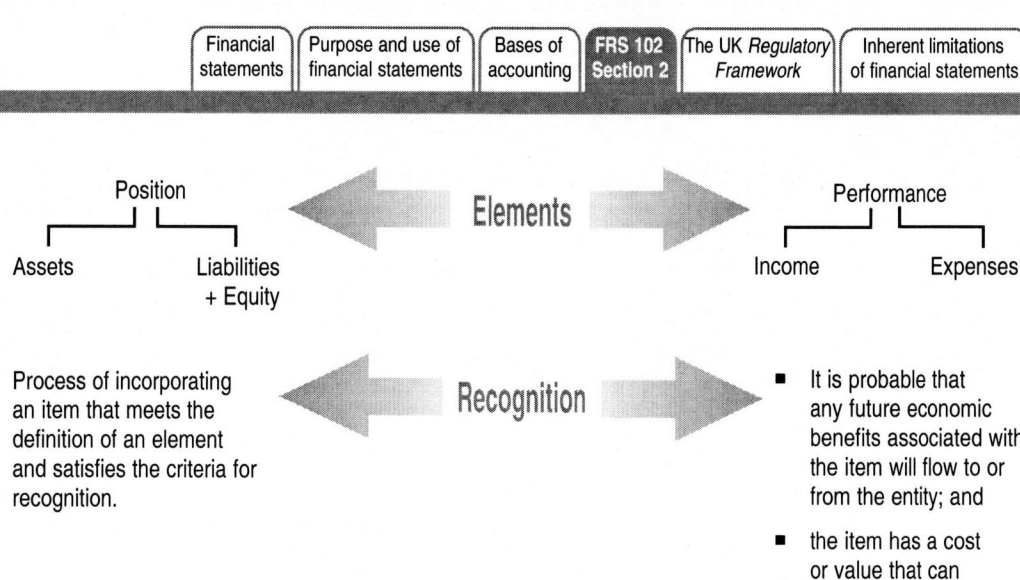

| Financial statements | Purpose and use of financial statements | Bases of accounting | FRS 102 Section 2 | **The UK *Regulatory Framework*** | Inherent limitations of financial statements |

UK Financial Reporting Standards (FRSs)100-105 are issued by the Financial Reporting Council (FRC).

UK companies must produce their financial statements in accordance with the Companies Act (CA 2006) and the applicable FRSs.

Listed UK companies must produce their consolidated financial statements in accordance with IFRS® Accounting Standards.

| Financial statements | Purpose and use of financial statements | Bases of accounting | FRS 102 Section 2 | The UK *Regulatory Framework* | **Inherent limitations of financial statements** |

Inherent limitations of financial statements

There are limitations inherent in the financial statements, including the fact that they are:

- a conventionalised representation, involving classification, aggregation and the allocation of items to particular accounting periods;
- historical (backward-looking); and
- based almost exclusively on financial data.

2: Ethics and sustainability

Topic List

Ethics

Sustainability

Ethics and sustainability are integrated throughout Financial Accounting and Reporting – UK GAAP. Ethical thinking must be the mainstay for honest, true, fair and prudent financial accounting and reporting. The application of sustainability knowledge and understanding is a key skill for all ICAEW Chartered Accountants.

Ethics | Sustainability

Code of Ethics

This lays out ICAEW's guidance on the ethics and behaviour required by all members and **students**. Guidance is in the form of **fundamental principles** (see below), specific guidance statements and explanatory notes.

Integrity	To be straightforward and honest in all professional and business relationships.
Objectivity	Not to compromise professional or business judgements because of bias, conflict of interest or undue influence of others.
Professional competence and due care	To attain and maintain professional knowledge and skill at the level required to ensure that a client or employing organisation receives competent professional service.
Confidentiality	To respect the confidentiality of information acquired as a result of professional and business relationships.
Professional behaviour	To comply with relevant laws and regulations and avoid any conduct that the professional accountant knows, or should know, might discredit the profession.

Compliance with the fundamental principles may potentially be threatened by a broad range of circumstances:

Threats

- **Self-interest** threat – financial interests, incentive compensation arrangements, undue dependence on fees.
- **Self-review** threat – data being reviewed by the same person responsible for preparing it.
- **Advocacy** threat – acting as an advocate on behalf of an assurance client in litigation or disputes with third parties.
- **Familiarity** threat – former partner of the firm being a director or officer of the client.
- **Intimidation** threat – threat of dismissal or replacement, being pressured to reduce inappropriately the extent of work performed in order to reduce fees.

Ethics | Sustainability

Two broad categories of safeguards which may eliminate or reduce threats to an acceptable level:

Safeguards created by the profession, legislation or regulation

For example:

- educational, training and experience requirements for entry into the profession
- continuing professional development requirements
- professional standards

Standards in the work environment

For example:

- organisation's ethics and conduct programmes
- strong internal controls
- leadership – stresses importance of ethics and expectation that employees will act in an ethical manner

| | Ethics | **Sustainability** |

Sustainability

- Reporting on **sustainability** – key part of a company's dialogue with stakeholders.
- In the UK:
  - **Strategic report** requires some disclosure of sustainability issues
  - **Task Force on Climate-related Financial Disclosures (TCFD)**

Impacts – how a company positively or negatively affects people and the planet.

Dependencies – reliance company has on environment, people and society.

Risks and opportunities usually come from dependencies but can also come from impacts.

Ethical considerations: When involved with preparing or reviewing sustainability disclosures, apply ethical principles – particularly integrity (no misleading information), professional behaviour (compliance) and professional competence and due care (do you have the skills/experience required to do the work?).

Ethics | **Sustainability**

IFRS Sustainability Disclosure Standards

IFRS S1 *General requirements for Disclosure of Sustainability-related Financial Information*

- Disclosure of information about all sustainability-related risks and opportunities that could reasonably be expected to affect the entity's prospects
- Information should be material, relevant and faithful representation
- Disclosures under 4 headings: governance, strategy, risks management and metrics & targets

IFRS S2 *Climate-related Disclosures*

- Disclosure of climate-related risks and opportunities
- Risks: transition risks and physical risks
- Disclosures under 4 headings: governance, strategy, risks management and metrics & targets
- Specified disclosures, eg around scope 1, 2 & 3 greenhouse gas (GHG) emissions

3: Format of financial statements

Topic List

Financial statements

Section 29 *Income Tax*

Statement of cash flows

This chapter covers the necessary material to help you to prepare useful financial statements. We start with a reminder of the formats for financial statements and then move onto additional areas.

| Financial statements | Section 29 *Income Tax* | Statement of cash flows |

ABC CO
BALANCE SHEET AS AT 31 DECEMBER 20X2

	20X2 £	20X2 £	20X1 £	20X1 £
Assets				
Fixed assets				
Intangible assets	X		X	
Tangible assets	X		X	
Investments	X		X	
		X		X
Current assets				
Stock	X		X	
Trade debtors	X		X	
Investments	X		X	
Cash at bank and in hand	X		X	
	X		X	
Creditors – amounts falling due within one year				
Trade creditors	X		X	
Finance lease liabilities	X		X	
	(X)		(X)	
Net current assets		X		X
Total assets less current liabilities		X		X
Creditors – amounts falling due after more than one year				
Finance lease liabilities	X		X	
Redeemable preference shares	X		X	
Borrowings	X		X	
Provisions	X		X	
		(X)		(X)
Net assets		X		X

ABC CO
BALANCE SHEET
AS AT 31 DECEMBER 20X2 (cont)

	20X2		20X1	
	£	£	£	£
Capital and reserves				
Called up share capital		X		X
Irredeemable preference share capital		X		X
Share premium account		X		X
Revaluation reserve		X		X
Profit and loss account		X		X
		X		X
Non-controlling interests		X		X
		X		X

ABC CO
PROFIT AND LOSS ACCOUNT
FOR THE YEAR ENDED 31 DECEMBER 20X2

	20X2 £	20X1 £
Turnover	X	X
Cost of sales	(X)	(X)
Gross profit	X	X
Other income	X	X
Distribution costs	(X)	(X)
Administrative expenses	(X)	(X)
Other expenses	X	X
Operating profit	X	X
Interest payable and similar expenses	(X)	(X)
Share of profit/(loss) of associates	X	X
Profit before tax	X	X
Tax on profit	(X)	(X)
Profit/(loss) for the financial year	X	X

ABC CO
STATEMENT OF COMPREHENSIVE INCOME FOR
THE YEAR ENDED 31 DECEMBER 20X2

	20X2 £	20X1 £
Profit/(loss) for the financial year	X	X
Other comprehensive income:		
Gains on property revaluation	X	X
Total comprehensive income for the year	X	X
Profit attributable to:		
Owners of the parent company	X	X
Non-controlling interests	X	X
	X	X
Total comprehensive income attributable to:		
Owners of the parent company	X	X
Non-controlling interests	X	X
	X	X

FRS 102 Section 29, *Income Tax*

Section 29 covers current tax. Current tax is fairly easy.

Tax charge

Current tax	X
Under-/over-statement of prior periods	X/(X)
	X

Current tax: an estimate of income tax payable for the current year.

Under-/over-statement of prior periods: as the income tax charge on taxable profits is only an estimate, there may be adjustments required in the next accounting period.

Indirect method

STATEMENT OF CASH FLOWS FOR YEAR ENDED 31.12.X1

Cash flows from operating activities

Net profit before tax	X
Adjustments for	
Depreciation	X
Investment income	(X)
Interest payable and other similar expenses	X
Operating profit before working capital changes	X
Increase in trade debtors	(X)
Decrease in stock	X
Decrease in trade creditors	(X)
Cash generated from operations	X
Interest paid	(X)
Income taxes paid	(X)
Net cash from operating activities	X

> Think carefully about what you are adding and subtracting.

	Financial statements	Section 29 *Income Tax*	Statement of cash flows

Net cash from operating activities brought forward — X

Cash flows from investing activities

Purchase of tangible fixed assets	(X)	
Proceeds from sale of tangible fixed assets	X	
Interest received	X	
Dividends received	X	
Net cash used in investing activities		(X)

Cash flows from financing activities

Proceeds from issue of share capital	X	
Proceeds from issue of long-term borrowings	X	
Payment of finance lease liabilities	(X)	
Dividends paid	(X)	
Net cash used in financing activities		(X)
Net increase in cash and cash equivalents		X
Cash and cash equivalents at beginning of period		X
Cash and cash equivalents at end of period		X

> **Cash equivalents:** short-term, highly liquid investments that are readily convertible to known amounts of cash and which are subject to an insignificant risk of changes in value.

Note: Cash and cash equivalents

Cash and cash equivalents consist of cash on hand and balances with banks, and investments in money market instruments. Cash and cash equivalents included in the cash flow statement comprise the following amounts.

	20X1 £m	20X0 £m
Cash on hand and balances with banks	X	X
Short-term investments	X	X
Cash and cash equivalents	X	X

Direct method

The operating activities section of the statement of cash flows is different.

	£'000
Cash flows from operating activities	
Cash receipts from customers	X
Cash paid to suppliers and employees	(X)
Cash generated from operations	X
Interest paid	(X)
Income taxes paid	(X)
Net cash from operating activities	X

| | | Financial statements | Section 29 *Income Tax* | **Statement of cash flows** |

Standard workings

TAX PAID

		Deferred tax b/d	X
∴ Tax paid	X	Income tax b/d	X
		Charge for year	X
Deferred tax c/d	X		
Income tax c/d	X		
	X		X

FINANCE LEASE LIABILITY

∴ Finance lease payments	X	B/d liability	
		< 1 year	X
		> 1 year	X
C/d liability		New finance lease in year	X
< 1 year	X		
> 1 year	X		
	X		X

FIXED ASSETS (carrying amount)

Bal b/d	X	Depreciation	X
Revaluation	X		
∴ Addition	X		
		Bal c/d	X
	X		X

Extra information

The statement of cash flows provides extra information not found in other primary statements.

- Relationships between profit and cash are shown.
- Cash equivalents are included in cash balances, giving a better picture of the liquidity of the company.
- Financing inflows and outflows must be shown, rather than simply passed through reserves.

Examining relationships

- **Cash flow gearing**: compare operating cash flows and financing flows, particularly borrowing.
- **Operating cash flows to investment flows**: match cash recovery from investment to investment.
- **Investment to distribution**: indicates the proportion of total cash outflow designated specifically to investor return and reinvestment.

Notes

4: Reporting financial performance

Topic List

- Accounting policies
- Discontinued operations
- Foreign currency
- Related parties
- Earnings per share
- Distributable profits
- IFRS Accounting Standards comparison

A number of different sections of FRS 102 provide guidance in different areas.

| Accounting policies | Discontinued operations | Foreign currency | Related parties | Earnings per share | Distributable profits | IFRS Accounting Standards comparison |

Section 10 *Accounting Policies, Estimates and Errors*

Accounting policies

Accounting policies are the specific principles, bases, conventions, rules and practices applied by an entity in preparing and presenting financial statements.

An entity follows extant Standards when determining its accounting policies.

In the absence of a Standard covering a specific transaction, other event or condition, management uses its judgement to develop an accounting policy which results in information that is relevant and reliable, considering in the following order:

- Standards dealing with similar and related issues
- Statements of Recommended Practice (SORPs) dealing with similar and related issues
- The definitions and recognition criteria set out in Section 2
- The requirements and guidance of UK-adopted IFRS Accounting Standards dealing with similar and related issues

Changes in accounting policy

Only allowed if:

- required by FRS; or
- if the change will provide more relevant or reliable information about events or transactions.

Accounting treatment:

- Restate prior year P/L and balance sheet.
- Restate opening balance of profit and loss reserves at start of earliest comparative period.
- Include as second line of statement of changes in equity of comparative period.
- Show effect on prior period at foot of prior year SOCIE.

Changes in accounting estimates

Apply **prospectively** ie, in the current period (and future periods if also affected).

| Accounting policies | Discontinued operations | Foreign currency | Related parties | Earnings per share | Distributable profits | IFRS Accounting Standards comparison |

Prior period errors

Omissions from and misstatements in the entity's financial statements for one or more prior periods.

Correct material prior period errors retrospectively in the first set of financial statements authorised for issue after their discovery.

- Restate comparative amounts for each prior period presented in which the error occurred.
- Restate the opening balances of assets, liabilities and equity (capital and reserves) for the earliest prior period presented.
- Include any adjustment to opening capital and reserves at the start of the earliest period presented as the second line of the statement of changes in equity.
- Disclose the nature of the error and the amount of the correction to prior periods for each line item in each period affected.

Where it is impracticable to determine the period-specific effects or the cumulative effect of the error, the entity corrects the error from the earliest period/date practicable (and discloses that fact).

Definitions

Discontinued operation	A component of an entity that has been disposed of and:
	- represents a separate major line of business or geographical area of operations;
	- was part of a single co-ordinated plan to dispose of a separate major line of business or geographical area of operations; or
	- was a subsidiary acquired exclusively with a view to resale.
Component of an entity	Operations and cash flows that can be clearly distinguished, operationally and for financial reporting purposes, from the rest of the entity.

| Accounting policies | **Discontinued operations** | Foreign currency | Related parties | Earnings per share | Distributable profits | IFRS Accounting Standards comparison |

The results of a discontinued operation should be present on the face of the profit and loss account in a **separate column**.

This column should show:

- the revenue, expenses and pre-tax profit or loss of discontinued operations;
- the related tax expense;
- the gain or loss on disposal;
- the related tax expense.

| Accounting policies | Discontinued operations | **Foreign currency** | Related parties | Earnings per share | Distributable profits | IFRS Accounting Standards comparison |

Two currency concepts

Functional currency

- Functional currency is the currency of the primary economic environment in which an entity operates.
- Functional currency is the currency used for measurement in the financial statements.
- All other currencies are treated as foreign currency.

Presentation currency

- This can be any currency.
- Special rules apply to translation from functional currency to presentation currency.
- The same rules are used for translating foreign operations.

4: Reporting financial performance

| Accounting policies | Discontinued operations | **Foreign currency** | Related parties | Earnings per share | Distributable profits | IFRS Accounting Standards comparison |

During the period

- Translate each transaction at **exchange rate on date of transaction** (average rate (AR) for a period may be used as an approximation, if rates do not fluctuate significantly).
- Where the transaction is settled during the period, the exchange difference arising is a realised gain or loss and is reported in profit or loss for the year.

At the reporting date

- **Non-monetary assets held at historic cost** (non-current assets, inventory): remain at historical rate (HR).
- **Non-monetary assets held at fair value** (eg, investments): exchange rate when fair value was determined.
- **Monetary assets and liabilities**: restate at closing rate.

Treatment of exchange differences

Part of profit/loss for the year:

- On **trading transactions**: under 'other operating income or expense'
- On **financing transactions**: under 'finance income/finance cost'

| Accounting policies | Discontinued operations | Foreign currency | **Related parties** | Earnings per share | Distributable profits | IFRS Accounting Standards comparison |

Related party

Person or **entity** related to reporting entity (RE):

(a) **Person** or close member of that person's family is related to RE if that person:
   - has **control** or **joint control** over RE; or
   - has **significant influence** over RE; or
   - is member of **key management** of RE or of a parent of RE.

(b) **Entity** is related to RE if any of following:
   - Entity and RE are in **same group**.
   - One entity is an **associate** or **JV** of other entity (or a member of group which other entity is a member of).
   - Both entities are **JVs** of same third party.
   - One entity is a **JV** of third party and other entity is an **associate** of the third entity.
   - Entity is **a post-employment benefit plan** for employees of either RE or entity related to RE.
   - Entity is **controlled/jointly controlled** by a **person** in (a).
   - Person with control/joint control over RE has **significant influence** or is a member of **key management** of the entity or a parent of the entity.
   - Entity, or any other group member, provides key management personnel services to the RE or its parent.

| Accounting policies | Discontinued operations | Foreign currency | **Related parties** | Earnings per share | Distributable profits | IFRS Accounting Standards comparison |

Disclosure (always required)	■ Related party relationship between parent/subsidiaries: parent's name and name of ultimate controlling party (if FS of parent or ultimate controlling party are not publicly available: disclose next most senior parent in group that does produce publicly available FS). ■ Key management personnel compensation in total and for short-term employee benefits, post-employment benefits, other long-term benefits, termination benefits, share-based payment.
Disclosure (only required if transactions in period)	■ Nature of the relationship ■ Amounts involved ■ Amount of any balances outstanding at year end ■ T&Cs attached to any outstanding balance ■ Details of any guarantees given/received ■ Any allowance against any outstanding balances and expense recognised in the period for bad or doubtful debts due from related parties ■ Disclosure of the fact that transactions were on an arm's length basis

IAS 33, *Earnings per Share*

This Standard aims to improve the **comparison** of different entities in the same period and of the same entity in different periods by requiring listed companies to disclose an Earnings per Share (EPS) on the face of the statement of profit or loss.

FRS 102 requires entities reporting under UK GAAP to comply with IAS 33 if they fall within its scope, so UK listed companies that have adopted UK GAAP must disclose the EPS for the year.

Basic calculation

$$\frac{\text{Net profit/loss attributable to ordinary shareholders}}{\text{Weighted average no. of shares in issue during the period}}$$

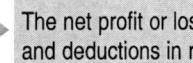

The net profit or loss used is after interest, tax and deductions in respect of non-equity shares.

| Accounting policies | Discontinued operations | Foreign currency | Related parties | **Earnings per share** | Distributable profits | IFRS Accounting Standards comparison |

Changes in capital structure

It is necessary to match the earnings for the year against the capital base giving rise to those earnings.

Bonus issue

The earnings of the entity will not rise (no new funds injected); to calculate the number of shares:

- Treat bonus shares as if in issue for the full year.
- Apply retrospectively, reducing the reported EPS for the previous year by the reciprocal of the bonus fraction.

Issue at full market price

New capital is introduced therefore earnings would be expected to rise from date of new issue; to calculate the number of shares:

- Use time weighted average number of shares for period.
- No retrospective effect.

Rights issue

For purposes of calculating the number of shares, treat this as an issue at full market price followed by a bonus issue:

- Use weighted average number of shares in issue for the period modified by the retrospective effect of the bonus element.
- Bonus element:

$$\frac{\text{Pre-rights FV of shares}}{\text{Theoretical ex-rights FV}}$$

Convertible loan notes or preference shares

- *Earnings*
  Net basis earnings X
  Add back loan note interest net of tax (or preference dividends) 'saved' X
  Diluted earnings X

- *No of shares*
  Basic weighted average X
  Add additional shares on conversion (use terms giving max dilution available after y/e) X
  Diluted number X

| Accounting policies | Discontinued operations | Foreign currency | Related parties | Earnings per share | **Distributable profits** | IFRS Accounting Standards comparison |

Distributable profits

- Private companies can distribute net accumulated realised profits.
- Traded or quoted companies can distribute net accumulated realised profits less net unrealised losses.

| Accounting policies | Discontinued operations | Foreign currency | Related parties | Earnings per share | Distributable profits | **IFRS Accounting Standards comparison** |

Under IFRS Accounting Standards (IFRS 5), a discontinued operation can be classified as such prior to disposal.

Under IFRS 5, discontinued operations are presented as a one-line entry on the face of the statement of profit or loss. The amount presented comprises:

- the profit or loss for the year of the discontinued operation;
- the related income tax expense;
- the profit or loss on disposal; and
- the related income tax expense.

This amount can be analysed on the face of the statement of profit or loss or in the notes.

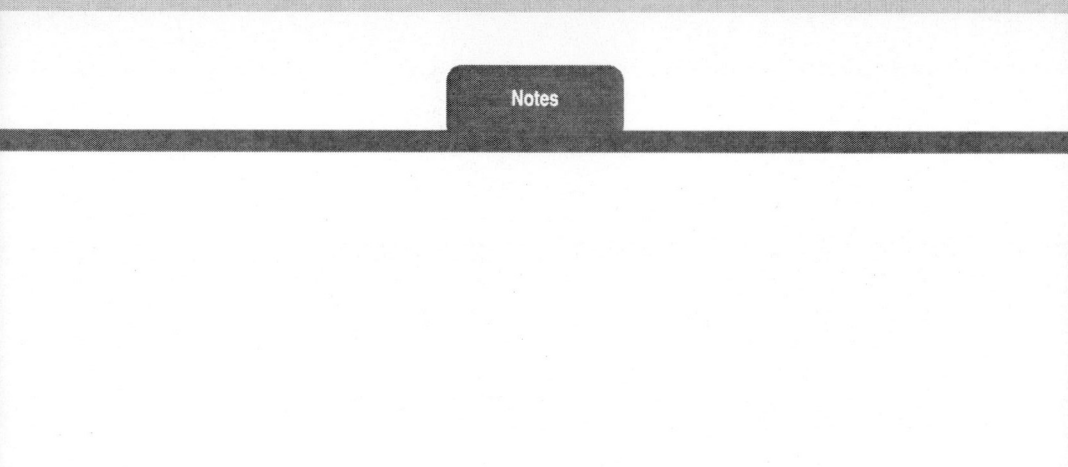

5: Tangible fixed assets

Topic List

Section 17

Borrowing costs

Depreciation

Impairment of assets

IFRS Accounting Standards comparison

Section 17 deals with most aspects of property, plant and equipment.

Depending on the nature of the business, these assets can have a significant impact on the financial statements. You also need to know how to deal with the impairment of fixed assets.

| Section 17 | Borrowing costs | Depreciation | Impairment of assets | IFRS Accounting Standards comparison |

Section 17 *Property, Plant and Equipment* covers all aspects of accounting for these items, which are most tangible fixed assets.

| Probable that future economic benefits associated with the asset will flow to the entity. | ⬅ **Recognition** ➡ | Cost of asset can be reliably measured. |

Initial measurement

Purchase price
- import duties
- non-refundable purchase taxes

less
- trade discounts/rebates

Directly attributable costs
- site preparation
- delivery/handling
- testing
- installation costs
- professional fees

Other costs
- estimate of unavoidable dismantling/removal costs and site restoration
- finance costs

Subsequent expenditure

Same criteria as initial costs. Otherwise do not capitalise but charge to profit or loss.

Subsequent measurement

Cost model	Revaluation model	Depreciation
- cost less accumulated depreciation and accumulated impairment losses	- revalued amount (fair value at the date of revaluation) less subsequent accumulated depreciation and impairment losses - revalue sufficiently regularly so carrying amount not materially different from fair value - all items of same class should be revalued	- systematic basis over useful life reflecting pattern of use of asset's economic benefits - periodic review of useful life, residual value and depreciation method and any change accounted for as change in accounting estimate

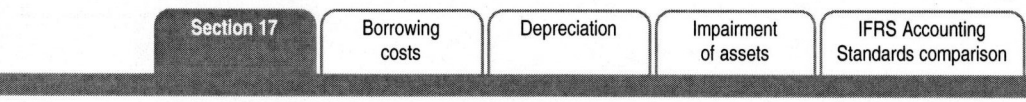

Changes in value on revaluation

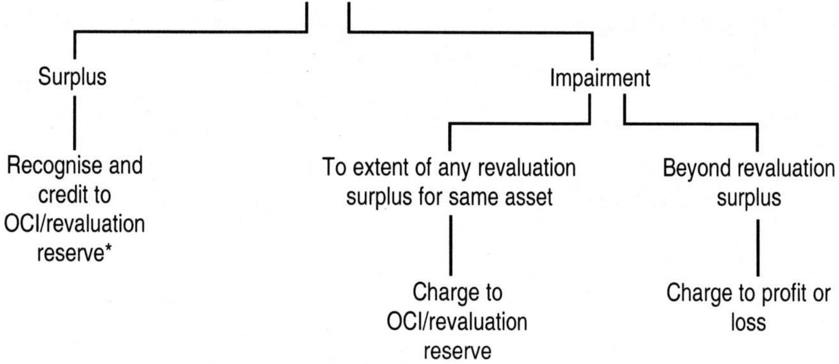

Surplus
- Recognise and credit to OCI/revaluation reserve*

Impairment
- To extent of any revaluation surplus for same asset
  - Charge to OCI/revaluation reserve
- Beyond revaluation surplus
  - Charge to profit or loss

*Unless reversing a previously recognised revaluation decrease of the same asset, in which case recognise as income to the extent of reversal of the previous decrease.

| Section 17 | **Borrowing costs** | Depreciation | Impairment of assets | IFRS Accounting Standards comparison |

Section 25 *Borrowing Costs*

This section deals with borrowing costs for **self-constructed assets** included in borrowing costs.

Borrowing costs: interest and other costs incurred by an entity in connection with the borrowing of funds.

- **Interest** on bank overdrafts and short and long term borrowings
- **Amortisation** of **discounts or premiums** related to borrowings
- **Amortisation** of arrangement **costs incurred**
- Finance charges in respect of **finance leases**
- **Exchange differences** as far as they are an adjustment to **interest costs**

Qualifying asset: an asset that necessarily takes a substantial period of time to get ready for its intended sale or use.

Capitalisation is allowed if the costs are **directly attributable** to the acquisition, construction or production of a qualifying asset. Entities can choose whether or not to capitalise borrowing costs.

| Section 17 | Borrowing costs | **Depreciation** | Impairment of assets | IFRS Accounting Standards comparison |

Depreciation

Depreciation is a means of allocating the **depreciable amount** of a tangible fixed asset to profit or loss over the useful life of the asset. It is an application of the accruals (matching) principle.

The annual depreciation charge on a fixed asset is based on two factors:

1 The **depreciable amount** of the asset. This is the amount which must be written off over the entire life of the asset. It consists of the original cost less any estimated residual value.

2 The **estimated useful life** of the asset. This may be measured in terms of years or in terms of units of service provided by the asset.

If an asset has to be revalued, the depreciation will be based on the revalued amount less residual value divided by the remaining useful life.

The double entry for depreciation is as follows.

DR Depreciation expense (P/L)
CR Accumulated depreciation (B/S)

This reflects:

- a periodic expense in profit or loss; and
- a decrease in the asset's carrying amount in the balance sheet.

Change in expected life

If after a period of an asset's life it is realised that the original useful life has been changed, then the depreciation charge needs to be adjusted.

The revised charge from that date becomes:

$$\frac{\text{Carrying amount at revised date}}{\text{Remaining useful life}}$$

Revaluation

A revaluation is recorded as follows:

DR Fixed asset
    (revalued amount less original cost)
DR Accumulated depreciation
    (total depreciation to date)
CR Revaluation reserve
    (revalued amount less carrying amount)

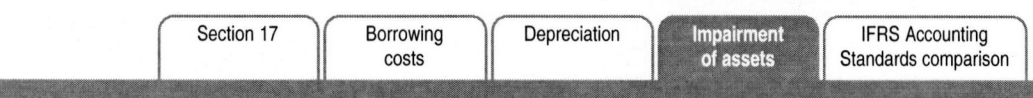

The aim of Section 27 *Impairment of Assets* is to ensure that assets are carried in the financial statements at no more than their **recoverable amount.**

Recoverable amount = higher of

Fair value less costs of disposal

- Amount obtainable from the sale of an asset in arm's length transaction less cost of disposal.

Value in Use (VIU)

- PV of estimated future cash flows expected to arise from the continuing use of an asset and its disposal at the end of its useful life.

Section 27 also specifies when an entity should reverse an impairment loss and prescribes certain disclosures for impaired assets.

Indicators of impairment

A review for impairment of a fixed asset or goodwill should be carried out if events or changes in circumstances indicate that the carrying amount of the fixed asset or goodwill may not be recoverable.

External indicators

- Fall in market value
- Change in technological, legal or economic environment
- Increase in market interest rate likely to affect discount rates
- Carrying amount of entity's net assets > market capitalisation

Internal indicators

- Obsolescence or physical damage
- Adverse changes in use
- Adverse changes in asset's economic performance

| Section 17 | Borrowing costs | Depreciation | Impairment of assets | **IFRS Accounting Standards comparison** |

IFRS Accounting Standards comparison

- Under IAS 16, proceeds arising from the sale of items produced during testing are taken to P/L; under FRS 102 such proceeds are deducted from the carrying amount of the item of PPE.

- There are no significant differences between IAS 36 and Section 27.

- Unlike FRS 102, IAS 23 does not allow entities to choose whether or not to capitalise borrowing costs. IAS 23 requires that borrowing costs directly attributable to a qualifying asset must be capitalised as part of the cost of that asset.

- IFRS 5 requires PPE which is to be disposed of to be reclassified as 'held for sale' subject to certain criteria. 'Held for sale' assets are subject to no further depreciation and are separately presented in the statement of financial position. There is no 'held for sale' category in UK GAAP.

6: Intangible fixed assets

Topic List

Section 18

Goodwill

IFRS Accounting Standards comparison

Section 18, Intangible Assets other than Goodwill prescribes the accounting treatment for intangible assets not dealt with under another section.

Goodwill is a controversial area. It comes up again in connection with group accounts.

| Section 18 | Goodwill | IFRS Accounting Standards comparison |

Definition

An intangible asset is an **identifiable** non-monetary asset without physical substance.

An intangible asset is **identifiable** if it is **separable** and/or it arises from **contractual or other legal rights**.

Recognition

Recognise if and only if:

- it is probable that the future economic benefits that are attributable to the asset will flow to the entity; and
- the cost of the asset can be measured reliably.

Initial measurement

Intangible assets should initially be measured at cost.

Subsequent expenditure

Subsequent expenditure must meet the original recognition criteria to be added to the cost of the intangible asset.

Amortisation

Should be charged on a systematic basis over the useful life of the asset. If unable to estimate the useful life reliably, then it should not exceed ten years. Should commence when asset available for use. Period and method to be reviewed at each year end.

Subsequent re-measurement

Cost model: cost less accumulated amortisation and impairment losses.

Revaluation model: revalued amount less subsequent accumulated amortisation and impairment losses.

- Revalued amount is fair value at date of revaluation by reference to an **active market**.
- All other assets in the same class should be revalued unless there is no active market for them, in which case the cost model value should be used for those assets.
- Regular revaluations so that the carrying value does not differ materially from fair value.

Section 18 | Goodwill | IFRS Accounting Standards comparison

Disclosures

Need to make the following disclosures:

- Distinguish between internally generated and other intangible assets
- Useful lives of assets and amortisation methods
- Carrying amount and accumulated amortisation at start and end of period
- Where the amortisation is included in the profit and loss account
- A reconciliation of opening balance to closing balance
- If research and development, how much was charged as expense

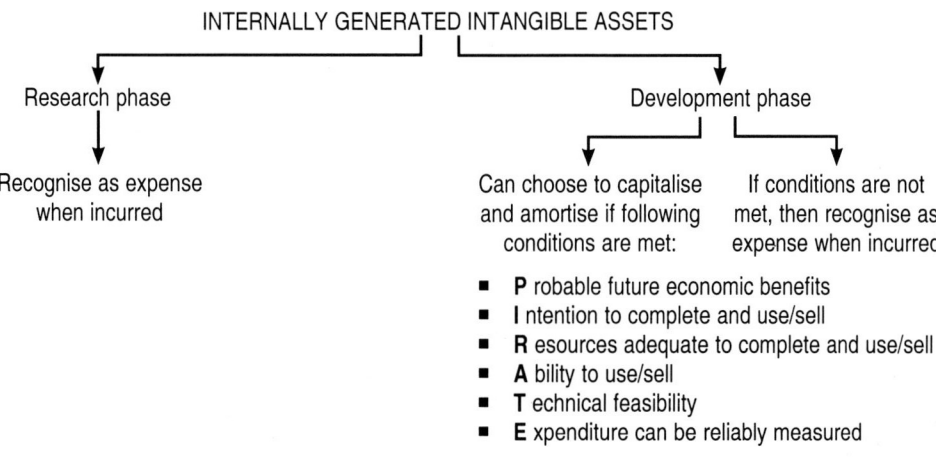

Internally generated brands, logos, publishing titles, customer lists and similar items should not be recognised as intangible assets.

| Section 18 | **Goodwill** | IFRS Accounting Standards comparison |

Goodwill can be purchased or be acquired as part of a business combination. In either case, the treatment is capitalisation.

Positive goodwill

Future economic benefits arising from assets that are not capable of being individually identified and separately recognised:

- Recognise as an **asset** and measure at cost/excess of purchase cost over interest in assets acquired and liabilities and contingent liabilities assumed.
- Amortise over its finite useful life. If unable to estimate useful life reliably, it should not exceed ten years.
- Test for **impairment** when indicators arise.

Negative goodwill

Arises when acquirer's interest in identifiable net assets exceeds the cost of the combination. Results from **errors** or a **bargain**:

- **Reassess cost** of combination and assets.
- Present on face of balance sheet as deduction from positive goodwill.

IFRS Accounting Standards comparison

- Under FRS 102, an entity can choose whether or not to capitalise development costs. IFRS Accounting Standards requires all eligible development costs to be capitalised.
- FRS 102 regards all intangible assets including goodwill as having a finite useful life, which cannot exceed ten years if the life cannot be estimated reliably. IAS 38 allows some intangible assets to be treated as having an indefinite useful life.
- FRS 102 requires goodwill to be amortised. IFRS 3 does not permit amortisation but requires goodwill arising on a business combination to undergo an annual impairment review.

7: Revenue and inventories

Topic List

Section 23

Section 13

Revenue recognition and the valuation of stock are important issues in ensuring that financial statements 'present fairly' the financial position and results of an entity.

Section 23

Revenue is the gross inflow of economic benefits during the period arising in the course of the ordinary activities of an entity when those flows result in increases in equity, other than increases relating to contributions from equity participants.

Revenue arises from sales, fees, interest, dividends and royalties.

Measurement

- Revenue should be measured at the **fair value** of the consideration received or receivable.
- Fair value will take into account any trade discounts and volume rebates allowed by the seller.

The reference to 'increases in equity' precludes the inclusion in revenue of amounts collected on behalf of others eg, sales tax (VAT in the UK) and amounts collected by agents on behalf of a principal.

Recognition

Sale of goods

Revenue should only be recognised when all of the following conditions are satisfied:

- The entity has transferred the significant risks and rewards of ownership of the goods to the buyer.
- The seller no longer has management involvement or effective control over the goods.
- The amount of revenue can be measured reliably.
- It is probable that the economic benefits associated with the transaction will flow to the entity.
- The costs incurred in respect of the transaction can be measured reliably.

Rendering of services

The outcome of a transaction can be estimated reliably when **all** of the following conditions are satisfied:

- The amount of revenue can be **measured reliably**.
- It is probable that the **economic benefits** associated with the transaction will flow to the entity.
- The **stage of completion** of the transaction at the end of the reporting period can be measured reliably.
- The **costs incurred** for the transaction and the **costs to complete** the transaction can be measured reliably.

Section 13

- Stock should be measured at the lower of cost and estimated selling price less costs to complete and sell (net realisable value); the comparison between the two should ideally be made separately for each item.
- Cost comprises all costs of purchase, costs of conversion and other costs incurred in bringing the stock to its present location and condition.
- Variable production overheads are absorbed into the cost of stock on the basis of actual levels of production; fixed production overheads are absorbed on the basis of normal levels of production.
- Stock can include raw materials, work in progress, finished goods, goods purchased and held for resale.
- FIFO and average cost are allowed.
- LIFO is not allowed.

- **Inventories** (stock) are assets:
  - held for sale in the ordinary course of business;
  - in the process of production for such sale; or
  - in the form of materials or supplies to be consumed in the production process or in the rendering of services.
- The estimated selling price is the price which that business expects to make from selling that inventory in the ordinary course of business, and is the price which is specific to that business.

8: Leases

Topic List

Lessee accounting

Sale and leaseback

Operating lease incentives

This chapter looks at lessee accounting, sale and leaseback transactions and operating lease incentives.

Lessor accounting is not in the syllabus.

| Lessee accounting | Sale and leaseback | Operating lease incentives |

Section 20 *Leases*

In a leasing transaction there is a contract between the lessor and the lessee for the right to use an asset.

Section 20 *Leases* standardises the accounting treatment and disclosure of assets held under lease. It follows the **substance over form** principle.

Finance lease
A lease that transfers substantially all the risks and rewards incidental to ownership of an asset from the lessor to the lessee.

Lease
An agreement whereby the lessor conveys to the lessee in return for a payment or series of payments the right to use an asset for an agreed period of time.

Operating lease
A lease other than a finance lease.

Accounting treatment for finance leases

Finance lease

When a lessee enters into a finance lease:

DR: Asset account
CR Creditors: Finance lease liabilities

Depreciation is charged on the asset:

DR: Depreciation expense
CR: Accumulated depreciation

Making the payment:

DR Creditors: Finance lease liabilities
CR: Cash

Finance charge:

The present value of the minimum lease payments is derived by discounting them at the interest rate implicit in the lease.

Interest is calculated and allocated to periods using the actuarial method.

DR P&L account: Interest cost
CR Creditors: Finance lease liabilities

| Lessee accounting | **Sale and leaseback** | Operating lease incentives |

Sale and leaseback transactions

- If the transaction is a sale and finance leaseback, the accounting entries are as follows:
  - Derecognise the carrying amount of the asset now sold.
  - Recognise the sales proceeds.
  - Calculate the profit on sale as proceeds less carrying amount and recognise it as deferred income.
  - Recognise the finance lease asset and the associated liability and measure them in the normal way (at the lower of fair value and the present value of the minimum lease payments).
  - Amortise the profit on sale as income over the lease term.

  The effect is to adjust the expense recognised in profit or loss for the period to an amount equal to the depreciation expense before the leaseback transaction.

- If the transaction is a sale and operating leaseback (where SP = sales proceeds and FV = fair value):
  - If SP = FV (an arm's length transaction), recognise any profit/loss immediately.
  - If SP < FV, recognise profit/loss immediately **unless** the apparent loss is compensated by future rentals at below market price, in which case defer and amortise.
  - If SP > FV, defer the excess over FV and amortise over the period for which the lease is expected to be used (ie, recognise FV minus carrying amount).

	Lessee accounting	Sale and leaseback	**Operating lease incentives**

- **Accounting treatment for operating leases**
  - **Balance sheet:** The balance sheet will only show accruals/prepayments in respect of the operating lease payments.
  - **Profit or loss account:** The lease payments under an operating lease are charged on a straight-line basis over the lease term. This applies even if the payments are not made on such a basis (for example, when the lessor provides incentives for the lessee to enter into a lease).

Notes

9: Financial instruments

Topic List

Liabilities and equity

Section 11 *Basic Financial Instruments*

Disclosures

IFRS Accounting Standards comparison

In recent years there has been a huge growth in the number and complexity of financial instruments available. This chapter considers the accounting requirements for these financial instruments.

| Liabilities and equity | Section 11 *Basic Financial Instruments* | Disclosures | IFRS Accounting Standards comparison |

Recent years have seen increasing use of a range of financial instruments.

Such instruments can have a significant effect on profits, solvency and cash flow.

The relevant sections of FRS 102 are:
- Section 22 *Liabilities and Equity*
- Section 11 *Basic Financial Instruments*

Definitions

Financial instrument: any contract that gives rise to a financial asset of one entity and a financial liability or equity instrument of another.

Financial asset: cash; equity instrument of another entity; contractual right to receive cash/other financial assets; contractual obligation to exchange financial instruments under potentially favourable conditions.

Section 22

- Financial instruments should be classified as either:
  - assets
  - liability (debt)
  - equity
- Compound instruments (exhibiting characteristics of both) must be split into their debt and equity components.
- Substance rather than legal form applies (eg, redeemable preference shares are a financial liability).
- Interest, dividends, loss or gains relating to a financial instrument classified as a liability are reported in profit or loss for the year, while distributions to holders of equity instruments are debited directly to equity (in the SOCIE).
- Offsetting of a financial asset and liability is only allowed where there is a legally enforceable right and the entity intends to settle net or simultaneously.

Financial liability: contractual obligation to deliver cash/other financial asset; contractual obligation to exchange financial instruments under potentially unfavourable conditions.

Equity instrument: contract that evidences a residual interest in the assets of an entity after deducting all its liabilities.

| Liabilities and equity | **Section 11 *Basic Financial Instruments*** | Disclosures | IFRS Accounting Standards comparison |

Section 11 Basic Financial Instruments

Recognition

- Financial instruments should be **recognised** when the entity becomes a **party to the contractual provisions of the instrument**.

Measurement

- Financial instruments are initially measured at **transaction price**, including transaction costs directly attributable to the acquisition or issue.
- Transaction costs are included in initial measurement (but not subsequent measurement).
- Subsequent measurement depends on classification.

Calculations – financial liabilities

The method used in the following example applies to deep discount bonds and other similar instruments (including zero coupon bonds).

> Debt issued for £400,000 (nominal) on 1.1.20X1 for proceeds of £315,526; redeemed for £400,000 (ie par) on 31.12.20X5
>
> Coupon rate = 4%
>
> Effective interest rate = 9.5%

Annual interest payments (4% × £400,000 × 5)	80,000
Deep discount £(400,000 – 315,526)	84,474
	164,474
At inception DR Cash £315,526	
CR Liability	£315,526

Subsequent measurement of such debt instruments should be at amortised cost, using the effective interest rate.

| | Liabilities and equity | Section 11 *Basic Financial Instruments* | Disclosures | IFRS Accounting Standards comparison |

Year	P/L charge *	Actual interest payable	Rolled up interest charged to P/L	Closing liability in B/S
20X1	29,975	16,000	13,975	329,501
20X2	31,303	16,000	15,303	344,804
20X3	32,756	16,000	16,756	361,560
20X4	34,348	16,000	18,348	379,908
20X5	36,092	16,000	20,092	400,000
	164,474	80,000	84,474	

*9.5% × opening liability in balance sheet

| Liabilities and equity | Section 11 *Basic Financial Instruments* | **Disclosures** | IFRS Accounting Standards comparison |

Disclosures required by Section 11

An objective of Section 11 is to require entities to provide disclosures in their financial statements that enable users to evaluate:

(a) the significance of financial instruments for the entity's financial position and performance; and

(b) the nature and extent of risks arising from financial instruments to which the entity is exposed and how the entity manages those risks.

This information can influence a user's assessment of the financial position and performance of an entity and of the nature of its future cash flows.

| Liabilities and equity | Section 11 *Basic Financial Instruments* | **Disclosures** | IFRS Accounting Standards comparison |

Disclosures

Balance sheet

- carrying amount and fair value of financial assets and liabilities
- reasons for any reclassification between fair value and amortised cost
- details of assets and exposure to risk where transfers of assets have taken place

Profit and loss account

- net gains/losses
- interest income/expense

| Liabilities and equity | Section 11 *Basic Financial Instruments* | Disclosures | **IFRS Accounting Standards comparison** |

IFRS Accounting Standards comparison

- Measurement after initial recognition under FRS 102 is generally amortised cost or fair value, whereas more categories exist under IFRS 9.

Notes

10: Other issues

Topic List

- Provisions and contingencies
- Events after the end of the reporting period
- Government grants
- IFRS Accounting Standards comparison

Provisions should be familiar to you from your earlier studies.

| **Provisions and contingencies** | Events after the end of the reporting period | Government grants | IFRS Accounting Standards comparison |

Section 21

Section 21 *Provisions and Contingencies* is based on IAS 37 which was brought in to remedy some abuses of provisions.

- Entities should **not provide** for **costs** that need to be incurred to **operate in the future,** if those **costs could be avoided** by the entity's future actions.
- **Costs of restructuring** are to be recognised as a provision only when the entity has an **obligation** to carry out the restructuring.
- The **full amount** of any **decommissioning costs** or environmental liabilities should be **recognised from the date on which they arise**.

Provision

A liability of uncertain timing or amount. Liabilities are obligations to transfer economic benefits as a result of past transactions or events.

Contingent liability

Should be disclosed unless the possibility of any outflow of economic benefits to settle it is remote.

Contingent asset

Should be disclosed where an inflow of economic benefits is probable.

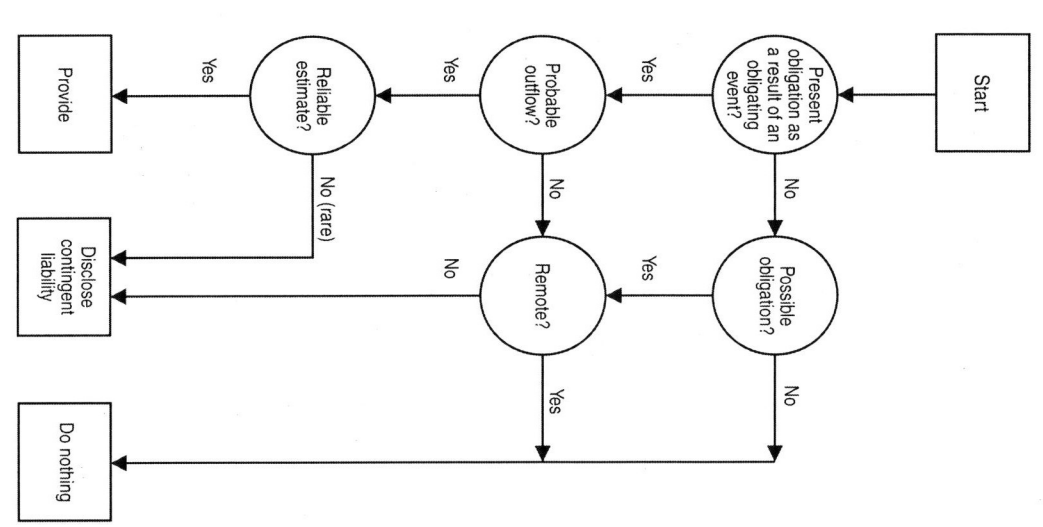

| Provisions and contingencies | **Events after the end of the reporting period** | Government grants | IFRS Accounting Standards comparison |

Section 32: Events after the End of the Reporting Period

Events, both favourable and unfavourable, which occur between the end of the reporting period and the date on which the financial statements are authorised for issue.

Adjusting events are events after the reporting period which provide additional evidence of conditions existing at the end of the reporting period, and therefore need to be incorporated into the financial statements.

Non-adjusting events are events which concern conditions which did **not** exist at the end of the reporting period.

Equity dividends proposed after reporting period: do not adjust but disclose.

An entity should not prepare its financial statements on a going concern basis if the management determines after the end of the reporting period either that it intends to liquidate its business, or to cease trading, or that it has no realistic alternative but to do so.

Examples

Adjusting events

- **fixed assets** – determination of purchase price or proceeds of sale
- **property and investments** – evidence of a permanent impairment
- **stock** – evidence of NRV
- **debtors** – renegotiation by or insolvency of trade debtors
- settlement of insurance claims
- discoveries of error or fraud
- **taxation** – rates fixed

Non-adjusting events

- mergers and acquisitions
- reconstructions
- issues of shares and debentures
- purchases/sales of fixed assets and investments
- loss or drop in value of fixed assets or stock occurring after the year end
- expansion or contraction of trade
- changes in rates of foreign exchange
- government action or strikes
- augmentation of pension benefits
- equity dividends declared after the reporting period

| Provisions and contingencies | Events after the end of the reporting period | **Government grants** | IFRS Accounting Standards comparison |

Section 24 *Government Grants*

Under Section 24 grants are recognised based on either the **performance model** or the **accrual model**.

Performance model

A grant that imposes performance-related conditions is recognised when those conditions are met.

If no conditions, it can be recognised on receipt.

If received before conditions are met it is recognised as a liability.

Accrual model

Grants relating to revenue are recognised over same period as related costs.

Grants relating to assets are recognised using the deferred income method.

IFRS Accounting Standards comparison

- IAS 20 allows a grant relating to assets to be recognised by deducting it from the carrying amount of the asset. This is not permitted under UK GAAP.

Notes

11: Analysis and interpretation of financial and non-financial information

Topic List

Accounting ratios

Non-financial performance measures

This chapter looks at the analysis and interpretation of financial and non-financial information for single entities, covering certain specified ratios and topics from an internal perspective.

| Accounting ratios | Non-financial performance measures |

Performance ratios

Performance ratios help a user to assess the company's ability to generate profit

Gross profit margin

Gross profit margin = $\dfrac{\text{Gross profit}}{\text{Turnover}} \times 100\%$

Reasons for changes vs prior year/other companies

Changes to turnover: change in sales price & cost stays same, change in sales mix, new products, currency translation

Changes to costs: change in cost & turnover stays same, efficiency improvements, economies of scale, inventory obsolescence, change in a/c policy (eg stock)

Operating profit margin

Operating profit margin = $\dfrac{\text{Operating profit}}{\text{Turnover}} \times 100\%$

Reasons for changes vs prior year/other companies

As for GP margin, plus: incurring non-recurring expenses (eg impairment loss), relocation costs, research costs, proportion fixed vs variable costs, improving operational efficiency

Efficiency ratios

> Efficiency ratios measure how effectively a company uses its assets and liabilities to generate sales and maximise profits

Asset turnover

measures how efficiently the company is using its assets to generate turnover.

$$\text{Asset turnover} = \frac{\text{Revenue}}{\text{Capital employed}}$$

Where:

Capital employed = equity + long-term liabilities, or total assets − short-term liabilities

Stock turnover/days

measures the **efficiency of managing stock levels relative to demand**

$$\text{Stock turnover} = \frac{\text{Cost of sales}}{\text{Stock}}$$

$$\text{Stock days} = \frac{\text{Stock}}{\text{Cost of sales}} \times 365$$

| Accounting ratios | Non-financial performance measures |

Efficiency ratios

Trade debtors collection period

measures in the number of days it takes credit customers to pay the company

$$\text{Trade debtors collection period} = \frac{\text{Trade debtors}}{\text{Turnover}} \times 365$$

Compare to company's credit policy, prior periods.

In general, shorter is better.

Trade creditors payment period

measures in the number of days it takes credit customers to pay the company

$$\text{Trade creditors payment period} = \frac{\text{Trade creditors}}{\text{Credit purchases}} \times 365$$

Trade creditors = valuable short-term finance, but delaying payment can cause operational problems if suppliers stop supplying until payment received

Gearing ratio

Gearing measures the proportion of a company's total capital structure that is financed by debt. It is a measure of risk.

$$\text{Gearing} = \frac{\text{Debt}}{\text{Equity}} \times 100\%$$

or

$$\text{Gearing} = \frac{\text{Debt}}{\text{Equity} + \text{debt}} \times 100\%$$

Debt = interest bearing non-current debt

In the exam, assume gearing = debt/equity unless told otherwise

Return on capital employed (ROCE)

ROCE measures how **efficiently** a company uses its resources (its capital employed) to generate profits.

$$\text{ROCE} = \frac{\text{Operating profit}}{\text{Capital employed}} \times 100\%$$

A company will want to **maximise** its ROCE.

ROCE is a useful ratio in analysing performance and efficiency together:

ROCE = operating profit margin × asset turnover

Breaking down ROCE into operating profit margin and asset turnover may help understand why ROCE has changed compared to prior years or other companies.

| Accounting ratios | Non-financial performance measures |

Considerations when interpreting accounting ratios

(a) Accounting treatments and judgements, eg revaluations of tangible fixed assets, useful lives, amortisation periods, measurement of provisions.

(b) Errors and deliberate incorrect accounting, eg a sudden or significant change in a ratio may indicate an error in the underlying data or inconsistency in the way transactions have been accounted for; ethical issues ‡ pressure to improve performance/position/not breach covenants?

(c) Economic issues, eg overall state of economy; interest rates, forex rates.

(d) Business issues ‡ type of business (eg services vs manufacturing ‡ different ROCE); management actions (eg price discounts, withdrawing from markets, efficiency projects).

Non-financial performance measures

Non-financial performance measures can help provide a better understanding of the company's performance and the value it creates.

Examples:

Customer-related: Net Promoter Score, Customer churn rate

Employee-related: Employee Net Promoter Score, Employee retention rate, Gender pay gap

Sustainability:

   Social: Diversity and inclusion measures, community contribution, social return on investment

   Environmental: Greenhouse gas emissions, progress towards net zero, water usage and management, energy use intensity

Others: eg cyber security, innovation measures, operational measures

Notes

12: Group accounts: basic principles

Topic List

Context for group accounts

The single entity concept

Control and ownership

Measurement of consideration

Non-controlling interests

Disclosure

This chapter introduces key principles of group accounting. Group accounts treat the individual companies of a group as a single economic entity.

| Context for group accounts | The single entity concept | Control and ownership | Measurement of consideration | Non-controlling interests | Disclosure |

Context for group accounts

A **group** is formed when one company buys shares in another company which gives it a **controlling** interest. Group accounts present the group as though it were a **single economic entity**.

Group accounts comprise:

- consolidated balance sheet
- consolidated profit and loss account and statement of comprehensive income
- consolidated statement of changes in equity
- consolidated statement of cash flows

| Context for group accounts | **The single entity concept** | Control and ownership | Measurement of consideration | Non-controlling interests | Disclosure |

Consolidation applies the single entity concept

Legal form		Economic substance
Each company is a separate legal person	⟷	The parent and subsidiaries are a single entity

Consolidated financial statements present a true and fair view of the group to the parent company shareholders.

| Individual parent company financial statements | | Consolidated financial statements |

Investment in subsidiary shown in balance sheet ⟶ Replaced by addition of subsidiary's net assets in consolidated balance sheet

Dividend income from subsidiary shown in profit or loss ⟶ Replaced by addition of subsidiary's revenue and costs in consolidated profit and loss account

| Context for group accounts | The single entity concept | **Control and ownership** | Measurement of consideration | Non-controlling interests | Disclosure |

Definitions

Subsidiary
An entity that is controlled by another entity known as the parent.

Control: the ability to govern the financial and operating policies of an entity so as to obtain benefit from its activities (FRS 102).

Associate
An entity in which an investor has significant influence and which is neither a subsidiary nor a joint venture of the investor.

Significant influence: the power to participate in the financial and operating policy decisions of an economic activity but not control over those policies.

A parent has **control** of a subsidiary but may not **own** 100% of it.

Summary of classification and treatment

Investment	Criteria	Required treatment in group accounts
Subsidiary	Control (>50% rule)	Full consolidation
Associate	Significant influence (20%+ rule)	Equity accounting
Joint venture	Joint control	Equity accounting
Investment which is none of the above	Assets held for accretion of wealth	As for single entity accounts

Group accounts reflect both **control** and **ownership**. The consolidated balance sheet shows the resources under group control and shows ownership split between the group and the non-controlling shareholders.

The treatment of these investments in the individual financial statements of the investor is dealt with in Section 9 *Consolidated and Separate Financial Statements*.

| Context for group accounts | The single entity concept | Control and ownership | **Measurement of consideration** | Non-controlling interests | Disclosure |

Deferred consideration

- To be payable at a later date.
- Measured at fair value at acquisition date.
- If payable in cash, discounted to present value.

Contingent consideration

- May be payable in the future.
- Recognised if probable and can be measured reliably.
- If amount paid is different to original estimate, Section 19 allows an adjustment to be made to the cost of the combination.

| Context for group accounts | The single entity concept | Control and ownership | Measurement of consideration | **Non-controlling interests** | Disclosure |

Measurement of NCI at acquisition date

Non-controlling interests are measured as share of the subsidiary's net assets at the date of acquisition.

Subsequent measurement of NCI

Carrying amount at the end of reporting period:

	£
NCI at acquisition	X
Share of post-acq profits and reserves	X
	X

| Context for group accounts | The single entity concept | Control and ownership | Measurement of consideration | Non-controlling interests | **Disclosure** |

Disclosure required in the separate financial statements of the parent includes a description of the methods used to account for its investments.

Disclosure required in the consolidated financial statements includes:

- basis for concluding that control exists when parent owns less than half the voting power;
- nature and extent of any significant restrictions on ability of subsidiaries to transfer funds to the parent; and
- name of any subsidiary excluded from consolidation and reason for exclusion.

13: Consolidated balance sheet

Topic List

Adjustments

Non-controlling interests

Goodwill arising on consolidation

Consolidated balance sheet

IFRS Accounting Standards comparison

The consolidated balance sheet provides the owners of the group with more information than is available in the parent company's own balance sheet. There are a number of standard adjustments with which you will become familiar.

| **Adjustments** | Non-controlling interests | Goodwill arising on consolidation | Consolidated balance sheet | IFRS Accounting Standards comparison |

Cancellation

When preparing a simple consolidated balance sheet:

- Take the individual accounts of the parent company and the subsidiary and cancel out items which appear as an asset in one company and a liability in another.
- Add together all the uncancelled assets and liabilities throughout the group.

Unrealised intra-group profit

This must be deducted from the profit of the company showing the profit. If this is the subsidiary, part of the adjustment will be made against the non-controlling interests.

Part cancellation

- The cost of investment may exceed the acquiree's share of the fair value of the assets acquired and liabilities and contingent liabilities assumed, raising the issue of goodwill.
- The parent may not have acquired all of the shares of the subsidiary, raising the issue of non-controlling interests.
- One entity may have issued loan stock a proportion of which is taken up by the other entity.

Acquisition part-way through the year

In this case, earnings for the year will have to be apportioned between the pre-acquisition and post-acquisition periods.

Tabs: Adjustments | **Non-controlling interests** | Goodwill arising on consolidation | Consolidated balance sheet | IFRS Accounting Standards comparison

Non-controlling interests

The interest in a subsidiary undertaking included in the consolidation that is attributable to the shares held by or on behalf of persons other than the parent.

Measuring NCI

NCI is measured using the proportionate basis ie, at the NCI's share of the fair value of the assets acquired, and liabilities and contingent liabilities assumed.

| Adjustments | Non-controlling interests | **Goodwill arising on consolidation** | Consolidated balance sheet | IFRS Accounting Standards comparison |

Goodwill working

	£	£
Consideration transferred		X
Less share of fair value of assets acquired and liabilities and contingent liabilities assumed:		
Share capital	(X)	
Profit and loss account reserves/other reserves	(X)	
Fair value adjustments	(X)	
Goodwill at acquisition		X
Amortisation to date		(X)
Goodwill at reporting date		X

Note that the subsidiary's profit and loss account will have to be apportioned if it is an acquisition part-way through the reporting period.

| Adjustments | Non-controlling interests | Goodwill arising on consolidation | **Consolidated balance sheet** | IFRS Accounting Standards comparison |

Summary: consolidated balance sheet

Purpose	To show the net assets which P controls and the ownership of those assets
Net assets	Always 100% P plus 100% S providing P controls S
Share capital	P only
Reason	Simply reporting to the parent company's shareholders in another form
Reserves	100% P plus group share of post-acquisition reserves of S less consolidation adjustments
Reason	To show the extent to which the group actually owns total assets less liabilities
Non-controlling interests	NCI share of S's consolidated net assets at the balance sheet date
Reason	To show the extent to which other parties own net assets that are under the control of the parent company

| Adjustments | Non-controlling interests | Goodwill arising on consolidation | Consolidated balance sheet | **IFRS Accounting Standards comparison** |

IFRS Accounting Standards comparison

- Under FRS 102, non-controlling interests is always measured on the proportionate basis. Under IFRS 3, it can be measured on acquisition at fair value or using the proportionate basis.
- Under FRS 102, acquisition-related costs are included in the consideration. Under IFRS 3, they are expensed.
- FRS 102 requires goodwill to be amortised over its finite useful life. If no reliable estimate of the useful life is possible, then a life of not more than ten years must be used. Under IFRS 3, goodwill is not amortised but reviewed annually for impairment.
- Under FRS 102, negative goodwill is recognised as a separate item within goodwill. Under IFRS 3, it is credited to profit or loss as a gain on a bargain purchase.
- FRS 102 allows a subsidiary to be excluded from consolidation due to severe long-term restrictions. IFRS 10 does not allow this.

14: Consolidated statements of financial performance

Topic List

Consolidated profit and loss account

Consolidated statement of changes in equity

Generally, the preparation of the consolidated profit and loss account is more straightforward to prepare than the consolidated balance sheet.

	Consolidated profit and loss account	Consolidated statement of changes in equity

Purpose	To show the results of the group for an accounting period as if it were a single entity.
Sales turnover to profit for the financial year	100% P + 100% S (excluding dividend receivable from subsidiary and adjustments for intra-group transactions).
Reason	To show the results of the group which were controlled by the parent.
Intra-group sales	Strip out intra-group activity from both turnover and cost of sales.
Unrealised profit on intra-group sales	(a) Goods sold by P: increase cost of sales by unrealised profit. (b) Goods sold by S: increase cost of sales by full amount of unrealised profit and decrease non-controlling interests by their share of unrealised profit.
Depreciation	If the value of S's fixed assets has been subjected to a fair value uplift then any additional depreciation must be charged in the consolidated profit and loss account. The non-controlling interests will need to be adjusted for their share.

Transfer of fixed assets	Expenses must be increase by any profit on the transfer and reduced by any additional depreciation arising from the increased carrying amount of the asset.
	The **net** unrealised profit (ie, the total profit on the sale less cumulative 'excess' depreciation charges) should be eliminated from the carrying amount of the asset and from the profit of the company that made the profit.
	For instance, H transfers an asset with a carrying value of £1,000 to S for £1,100. Depreciation is 10% pa. The net unrealised profit is £90. This is debited to H's profit and loss and credited to the carrying amount of the asset.
Non-controlling interests	NCI% × S's profit for the financial year.
Mid-year acquisition	Apportion profit and loss account of subsidiary between pre-acquisition and post-acquisition periods.

| **Consolidated profit and loss account** | Consolidated statement of changes in equity |

Consolidated profit and loss account

Adjustments required

- Eliminate **intra group sales and purchases**.
- Eliminate **unrealised profit** on intra group purchases still in stock at the year end.
- Eliminate **intra group dividends**.
- Show the NCI as a separate line after profit for the financial year.

> Unrealised profit and losses:
>
> Only where S sells to P, allocate the unrealised profit between NCI and P: Debit group profit and loss reserves, Debit NCI, Credit stock

Procedure

- **Combine all P and S results** from sales turnover to profit after tax for the financial year. Time apportion where the acquisition is mid-year.
- Exclude **intra group investment** income.
- **Calculate NCI** (NCI% × S's PFY).

| Consolidated profit and loss account | **Consolidated statement of changes in equity** |

Consolidated statement of changes in equity

As with the single company statement, this is a link between the consolidated profit and loss account and the equity section of the consolidated balance sheet. Here is a very simple example:

Consolidated profit and loss account extract 20X9

	£'000
Profit after tax	572
Profit attributable to:	
Owners of parent	531
Non-controlling interests	41
	572

Note: Dividends paid during the year were as follows:

Parent: £97,000
Subsidiary: £26,000 to NCI

Consolidated balance sheet extract

	20X8 £'000	20X9 £'000
Share capital	600	600
Share premium	70	70
Retained earnings	324	758*
	994	1,428
Non-controlling interests	121	136**
	1,115	1,564

* (324 + 531 − 97)
** (121 + 41 − 26)

Consolidated profit and loss account | **Consolidated statement of changes in equity**

Consolidated statement of changes in equity

	Share capital £'000	Share premium £'000	Profit and loss account reserves £'000	Total £'000	Non-controlling interests £'000	Total £'000
Balance at 1 January 20X9	600	70	324	994	121	1,115
Total comprehensive income for the year			531	531	41	572
Dividends paid			(97)	(97)	(26)	(123)
Balance at 31 December 20X9	600	70	758	1,428	136	1,564

15: Associates and joint ventures

Topic List

Equity method

Transactions with associates

Joint ventures

IFRS Accounting Standards comparison

An associate or joint venture is accounted for using the equity method.

| **Equity method** | Transactions with associates | Joint ventures | IFRS Accounting Standards comparison |

Individual investor's accounting records

- Carry at cost
- At fair value

Balance sheet

Initial cost	X
Add/less post acquisition share of profits/losses (before dividends)	X/(X)
Less post-acquisition dividends received to avoid double counting	(X)
Carrying amount	X

Consolidated financial statements

Use equity method unless:

- investment acquired and held exclusively with a view to disposal soon; and
- investor ceases to have significant influence.

In these cases record at cost.

Profit and loss account

Group share of associate's profit for the year

Note that where the associate makes a **loss** this is recognised in the group profit or loss and deducted from the carrying amount of the associate.

| Equity method | **Transactions with associates** | Joint ventures | IFRS Accounting Standards comparison |

Associates are not part of the group so trading transactions are **not** cancelled on consolidation.

Items requiring adjustment

- Unrealised profit on transactions between group and associate should be eliminated.
- Loans and trading balances between group and associate should be shown separately.
- Dividend income from the associate is not included in the consolidated profit and loss account.

Items not requiring adjustment

- Turnover and cost of sales are not adjusted for trading between group and associate.
- Debtor and creditor balances are not cancelled.

| Equity method | Transactions with associates | **Joint ventures** | IFRS Accounting Standards comparison |

Joint ventures

A joint venture is a contractual arrangement whereby two or more parties undertake an economic activity that is subject to joint control.

Joint control

Is the contractually agreed sharing of control of an arrangement, which exists only when decisions about the relevant activities require the unanimous consent of the parties sharing control.

Accounting treatment

In the consolidated accounts joint ventures are accounted for using the **equity method**.

			IFRS Accounting Standards comparison
Equity method	Transactions with associates	Joint ventures	

- Implicit goodwill is recognised and amortised upon acquisition of an associate or joint venture under FRS 102. No implicit goodwill is recognised under IAS 28.
- FRS 102 requires less detailed disclosures about investments in associates and joint ventures than IFRS 12.

Notes

16: Group accounts: disposals

Topic List

Disposals

Discontinued operations

The Financial Accounting and Reporting syllabus only covers full disposal of subsidiaries.

| | Disposals | Discontinued operations |

Note: Goodwill on acquisition which has not been written off by amortisation or impairment must be included in the calculation of of profit/loss on disposal.

Gain or loss on disposal is calculated as follows:

In holding company accounts

	£
Sales proceeds	X
Less cost of investment	(X)
Profit/(loss)	X/(X)

In group accounts

	£	£
Sales proceeds		X
Carrying amount of gooodwill at disposal:		
Goodwill at acquisition	X	
Impairment	(X)	
		(X)
Share of net assets at disposal		(X)
Profit/(loss) on disposal		X

Disposal

- In CPL:
  - Consolidated results to date of disposal
  - Show group profit or loss on disposal separately before interest
- In CBS: no subsidiary therefore no consolidation or NCI

Note: A subsidiary disposed of will usually qualify to be treated as a **discontinued operation**.

	Disposals	Discontinued operations

Dividends

The retained earnings/net assets at the date of disposal of the subsidiary are calculated deducting **only** dividends to which the parent company is entitled ie, dividends paid up to the date of disposal.

Pro-forma calculation at the date of disposal:	
Profit and loss reserves brought forward	X
Profit for the year to date of disposal	X
Dividends paid at date of disposal	(X)
	X

Disclosure

- The profit or loss on disposal should be presented separately where significant.
- Additional disclosure may be required if the sale is classed as a discontinued operation.

| | Disposals | **Discontinued operations** |

Definitions

Discontinued operation	A component of an entity that has been disposed of and:
	(a) represented a separate major line of business or geographical area of operations;
	(b) was part of a single co-ordinated plan to dispose of a separate major line of business or geographical area of operations; or
	(c) was a subsidiary acquired exclusively with a view to resale.
Component of an entity	Operations and cash flows that can be clearly distinguished, operationally and for financial reporting purposes, from the rest of the entity.

The results of a discontinued operation must be presented in a separate column on the face of the profit and loss account, as explained in Chapter 3 earlier.

Notes

17: Group statement of cash flows

Topic List

Section 7

Consolidated statements of cash flows

The work involved in preparing a group statement of cash flows is very similar to that involved in preparing an individual entity statement of cash flows. However, there are a number of additional issues to be considered.

Section 7 | Consolidated statements of cash flows

Section 7 format

Inflows and outflows of cash of an entity are classified between the major economic activities:

- operating activities
- investing activities
- financing activities

Section 7 requires the following notes:

- **Non-cash transactions**: these are obviously excluded from the statement of cash flows but must be separately disclosed if necessary for an understanding of the entity.
- **Components of cash and cash equivalents**: amounts b/f and c/f must reconcile to amounts in the balance sheet.

Definitions

Cash: cash on hand and demand deposits.

Cash equivalents: short-term highly liquid investments that are readily convertible to known amounts of cash and which are subject to an insignificant risk of changes in value (generally < three months maturity).

What is a statement of cash flows for?

Information on cash flows assists the user in assessing an entity's viability.

- Shows entity's cash generating ability
- Shows entity's cash utilisation needs

The statement required by Section 7 is based on movement in cash and cash equivalents and can be criticised for not focusing on 'pure' cash.

Consolidated cash flows

Extra notes are required under investing activities:

- purchase or disposal of subsidiary;
- purchase or disposal of other business units.

Non-controlling interests

Only the actual payment of cash, eg, dividends to non-controlling shareholders, should be reflected in the statement of cash flows. Include under 'cash flows from financing'.

NON-CONTROLLING INTERESTS			
	£		£
NCI dividend paid (balancing figure)	X	b/f NCI (CBS)	X
c/f NCI (CBS)	X	NCI (CP&L)	X
	X		X

Section 7 | Consolidated statements of cash flows

Associates and joint ventures

Only the actual cash flows from sales or purchases between the group and the entity, and investment in and dividends from the entity should be included.

- Dividends received should be included as a separate item in 'cash flows from investing activities'.
- Separate disclosure of cash flows relating to acquisitions and investments.
- Separate disclosure of financing cash flows between the reporting entity and equity-accounted investees.

INVESTMENTS IN ASSOCIATES		
	£	£
b/f Inv in Associate (CBS)	X	Dividend received (balancing figure) X
Share of profit of Associate (CP&L)	X	c/f Inv in Associate (CBS) X
	X	X

Acquisition or disposal of a subsidiary

Present as a simple item of cash inflow or outflow.

- Cash paid/received as consideration should be shown **net** of any cash transferred as part of the purchase/sale.
- Summary note required showing:
  - total purchase/disposal consideration
  - portion that was cash/cash equivalents
  - cash/cash equivalents acquired/disposed of
  - other assets/liabilities acquired/disposed of

Notes

18: Micro-entities

Topic List

The micro-entities regime

FRS 105 financial statements

FRS 105 – FRS 102 comparison

Very small entities can now report under FRS 105 The Financial Reporting Standard applicable to the Micro-entities Regime.

| The micro-entities regime | FRS 105 financial statements | FRS 105 – FRS 102 comparison |

The Micro-entities regime

The micro-entities regime offers a simplified set of reporting requirements designed to reduce the administrative burden on small entities.

Criteria to qualify as a micro-entity:

- Turnover not above £632,000.
- Balance sheet total not in excess of £316,000.
- No more than 10 employees.
- Plcs or companies that prepare consolidated financial statements are not permitted to apply FRS 105.

| | The micro-entities regime | **FRS 105 financial statements** | FRS 105 – FRS 102 comparison |

FRS 105 financial statements

Balance sheet format 1 – net assets basis (Section 4.3)

	£	£
Called-up share capital not paid		X
Fixed assets		X
Current assets	X	
Prepayments and accrued income	X	
Creditors: amounts falling due within one year	(X)	
Net current assets (liabilities)		X/(X)
Total assets less current liabilities		X
Creditors: amounts falling due after more than one year		(X)
Provisions for liabilities		(X)
Accruals and deferred income		(X)
		X
Capital and reserves		X

	The micro-entities regime	**FRS 105 financial statements**	FRS 105 – FRS 102 comparison

Balance sheet format 2 – vertical presentation

Assets
  Called up share capital not paid   X
  Fixed assets   X
  Current assets   X
  Prepayments and accrued income   <u>X</u>
                                                                <u><u>X</u></u>

Capital, Reserves and Liabilities
  Capital and reserves   X
  Provisions for liabilities   X
  Creditors
    Amounts falling due within one year   X
    Amounts falling due after one year   <u>X</u>
                                                                X
  Accruals and deferred income   <u>X</u>
                                                                <u><u>X</u></u>

Profit and loss account

The format of the profit and loss account is as follows: (FRS 105 Section 5.3)

	£
Turnover	X
Other income	X
Cost of raw materials and consumables	(X)
Staff costs	(X)
Depreciation and other amounts written off assets	(X)
Other charges	(X)
Tax	(X)
Profit or loss	X/(X)

Note that FRS 105 requires expenses to be classified by **nature** rather than function.

There is no requirement for separate disclosure in respect of discontinued operations.

| | The micro-entities regime | FRS 105 financial statements | **FRS 105 – FRS 102 comparison** |

FRS 105 – FRS 102 comparison

	FRS 105	**FRS 102**
Group accounts	No group accounts prepared. Investments in other entities accounted for under Section 9 *Financial Instruments*.	Group accounts prepared.
Financial instruments	Initially measured at cost +/- transaction costs. No remeasurement or use of fair value. No use of effective interest rate.	Can be measured at fair value if criteria met. Amortised cost uses effective interest rate.
Property, plant and equipment	Measured at cost less depreciation/ impairment. No revaluation.	Revaluation is allowed if applied to all assets in a class.
Borrowing costs	Recognised as an expense in the period.	May be capitalised in respect of qualifying asset.
Development costs	Recognised as an expense in the period.	Option to capitalise if criteria met.
Government grants	Must use accrual model.	Accrual or performance model permitted.

19: IFRS Accounting Standards overview

Topic List

Financial statements

Group accounts

Other issues

In this chapter we look at financial reporting requirements under IFRS Accounting Standards and how these differ from UK GAAP as set out in FRS 102 and CA 2006.

	Financial statements	Group accounts	Other issues

Financial statements

- The statement of financial position format in IAS 1 is not presented on a net assets basis.
- Under IAS 1, an entity can present a single statement of comprehensive income or a statement of profit or loss and statement of comprehensive income.
- Under FRS 102, an entity can in certain circumstances present a **statement of income and retained earnings** in place of the (separate) statement of comprehensive income and statement of changes in equity. This does not exist in IFRS Accounting Standards.
- The statement of cash flows in IAS 7 follows the same format as UK GAAP.